MY *PRESS* TO PRAISE!

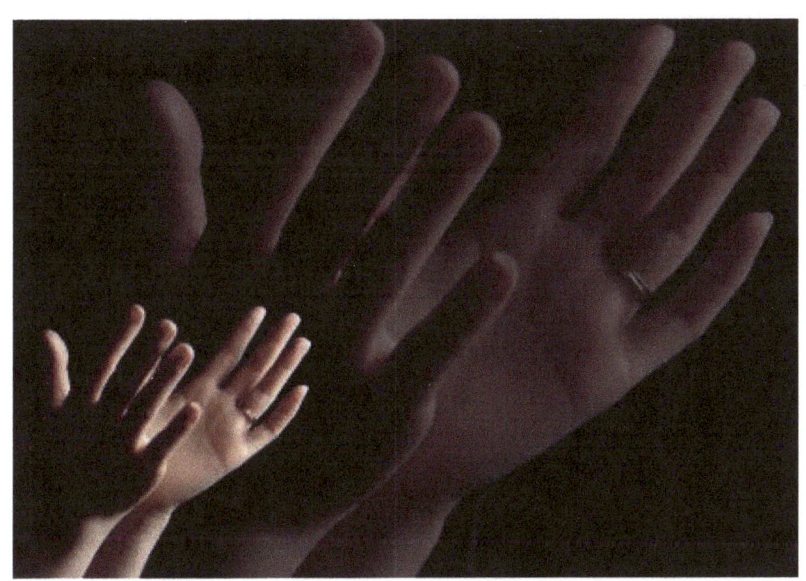

TERESA A. STITH

My Press to Praise

Copyright © 2022 Teresa A. Stith

All rights reserved. This book is protected by the copyright laws of the United States of America. This book may not be copied or reprinted for commercial gain or profit. The use of short quotations or occasional page copying for personal, or group study is permitted and encouraged. Permission will be granted upon request.

Unless otherwise identified, scripture quotations are from the King James Version of the Bible. Copyright © 1982 by Thomas Nelson, Inc. Used by permission. All rights reserved.

Please note that certain pronouns referring to the Father, Son, and Holy Spirit may be capitalized to acknowledge God and any such titles referring to Him. Please note just the opposite when referring to satan. We choose not to capitalize his name or acknowledge him in any way, even to the point of violating grammatical rules.

ISBN-13: 978-1-7332744-4-9

Publisher- A Faith That Works Publishing

Website: afaiththatworks.com

Why has it become so hard to *press*? ***EVERYTHING*** is a *press*. When we wake up in the morning, we *press* to get out of bed. We *press* to get ready for work, *press* to pray, *press* to read God's word, *press* to fast, and *press* to go to church. We find energy for everything else that we want to do, but when it comes to God, we find ourselves not having the drive, the motivation, the strength, or the time to *press* forward in Him. We have become so lazy, distracted, and bothered by life, that it's a *press* just to maintain some sort of focus. In all reality, we are losing ourselves in what is happening in the world. Laws and other things are changing so rapidly that we are becoming mentally challenged or literally forced to keep up with all that is transpiring. Listen, do not allow yourself to get caught up in the hype. Everything that is happening in this season is a ploy of the enemy to keep you so focused on what is going on in the world, that you are not paying attention to God or the signs of the times. Jesus is soon to come, so don't be so consumed with the issues and troubles of the world, that you miss the call to "come out from among them, and be ye separate (set apart) saith the Lord, and touch not the unclean thing; and I will receive you" (2 Corinthians 6: 17).

The bible urges us to PRESS toward the mark for the prize of the high calling of God in Christ Jesus (Philippians 3:14). If you don't do anything else my dear brothers and sisters, you must *PRESS* your way through! **Only those** who endure unto the end shall be saved! (Matthew 24:13).

TITLES BY TERESA STITH

A FAITH THAT WORKS

THE REAL PURPOSE BEHIND THE HAT

LIVE LIKE YOU KNOW

STEP

LOVE PSALMS TO GOD FOR MY HUSBAND

THE ROAD THAT LEADS TO FREEDOM

The eyes of **ALL** look **EXPECTANTLY**

to You, and **YOU**

give them their food in **DUE** season!

Psa. 145:18

For we know that the whole creation groaneth and

travaileth in pain together until now.

And not only so, but ourselves also,

which have the first fruits of the Spirit,

even we ourselves groan within ourselves,

waiting for the adoption, to wit,

the redemption of our body.

Romans 8:22-24

The Most Expensive

thing that we can

offer unto God

is our

PRAISE!

INTRODUCTION

I had a dream, and in the dream, I saw gold hearts floating across the sky. These weren't just any ole' hearts, they were *perfect* gold hearts and each one was clothed with fire. One after another, they floated in sync with each other along the sky. I was absolutely amazed, as I had never seen a *perfect heart* before. Suddenly, there appeared a man whom I perceived to be Christ or One like the Son of man, who stepped out from behind the clouds and gave a command by raising his right hand. When He raised his right hand, those hearts began to race across the sky (still in sync with one another) and then forming this phrase **"WHERE IS MY PRAISE?"** I was so completely blown away by such a humble display of authority and power, that I have put into this book the Lord's message that we should *PRESS* to praise Him regardless of our personal life's challenges. The bible declares that God inhabits the praises of His people (Psalm 22:3). Praising God means to tell of the

Lord's goodness in your life by rejoicing and being exceedingly GLAD! (Matthew 5:12). We are drawn by the Spirit of God into His presence when we humble ourselves, pray, and seek God's face. Whether we are singing, dancing, or teaching others, however we are using our gifts to glorify God, the Lord is pleased with our sacrifices. The thing that blesses me the most about praise is that God recognizes these forms of expression when they come from a sincere place in us. Remember, He's looking for TRUE worshippers! When we open our hearts to God in love, He fills us with more of Himself, and He continues to do so as we continue to make ourselves available. As we continue to make ourselves available, we find that we began to *become* more like Him! We think like Him, we behave like Him, we began to develop His mind which allows us to come to know His thoughts and plans for our lives and the lives of those around us. We began to talk like Him, and act like Him, everything becomes about HIM!

      Having an attitude of praise takes practice. Not

an empty ritual of some sort, but genuine transformation or transferring of your will to the will of God for your life. With all that is within you, let your praise flow from a heart filled with thanks. Worship the Lord with the "the fruit of your lips." What kind of fruit do you have on your lips today? As you consider this, **think** before you speak! If we learn to be mindful that "fruit" should be constantly flowing from our hearts to our lips, we would be more careful and considerate, and not waste words. The Bible says that "every idle word that men shall speak, they shall give account thereof in the day of judgement" (Matthew 12:36). When we magnify and glorify the Lord, the focus of our lives shifts from our troubles to His goodness (the Holy Spirit). The Bible tells us that even the plants groan and travail waiting for that blessed hope that is in Christ Jesus. Listen, our redemption is a future redemption and even though we have been redeemed already by the precious blood of Jesus Christ, we await the FULL accomplishment of that redemption when Jesus returns to receive us unto Himself. HE HAS BEEN MORE than enough for us, and our praise is our reasonable service to Him. If you have made the Lord your trust, praise happens. In God's eyes, it is fair, attractive, and pleasant to look at. When you've had an encounter with the Holy Spirit, praise goes beyond mere words being spoken, and you begin to live a life that is exemplified through holiness. Your behavior changes, and you begin to learn what it means to be obedient. Your desire is to please God. Period.

In *"My Press to Praise"* we understand that even when we don't *feel* like praising God, we must. We have become accustomed to only praising God when things are going well for us, but I remember my First Lady asking this question in a women's meeting one day, stating "what will you do when God flips it?" Meaning, if you center or build your life around the *stuff* that you acquire or upon things that the world promises to provide for you, what will you do if God allows this to no longer be an option for you? Can you still find praise when circumstances shift and the heat and weight of trials comes to test your faith? Can you still praise God when things aren't going in your favor? This life's journey is seen crushing and swallowing people up every day with its pressures and worries, and praise helps us to plant our feet and endure. We should always be willing to sacrifice a praise to the Lord for all the wonderful works that He has wrought in our lives time and time again. Your "Press to Praise" is simply making a conscious decision to trust in God regardless of what you see or think about your current situation. God takes praise very seriously, for this is why we were created, to bring glory and honor to His name, to worship Him and learn of Him. It is most rewarding to know that others can find Christ simply through your life, your witness, and your acts of worship. Your testimonies of praise to the Lord helps others to build their own strength and confidence in how they look at life and how they should respond when situations look hopeless.

      How we respond to pressing issues can have a

grave impact on someone else's ability to go through and come out victoriously. It can also prove to be very helpful for those who may have doubted God in the past. Listen, when you are down to nothing, God is always up to something! He uses the hard things in life not only to get our attention and draw us closer to Him, but to build character in us. If you're honest with yourself, our troubles have been the driving force that we needed to mend our relationship with the Lord. When we face something that is bigger than us, we tend to look to SOMEONE who is also bigger than us. Many who were not fully persuaded about who God is, have found themselves calling on Him in times of trouble. The Bible declares that every knee shall bow and every tongue shall confess that Jesus Christ is Lord (Philippians 2:10-11).

WHERE IS *YOUR* PRAISE?

TABLE OF CONTENTS

1. Resolving to ENDURE..................................1
2. Your APPROACH to Praise.......................9
3. The PRESS in Your Praise....................…..23
4. Make TIME to Praise................................…..33
5. A SHIFT in Worship and Praise...................43
6. Get a New HEART....................................53
7. Now THINK on These Things....................59
8. For Thought...64
9. About the Author......................................65
10. Upcoming Titles.…...................................67
11. References..70

COME OVER HERE

where the table is spread

AND THE FEAST OF THE LORD

is going on!

Luke 14: 15-22

My Press to Praise

Resolving to Endure

(1)

This has definitely been a season of endurance for me. Aside from dealing with the pressures of the daily work environment, I've had to endure spiritual attacks in my dreams as I slept. The enemy has stepped up his game and is changing the way that he wars against the saints. I hope that you are paying attention. He is using different approaches and strategies in this season, in an effort to wear out the saints of God, but God has given us the tools that we need to combat him. The only power that the enemy has to use against us, is that which we have given to him. He is powerless. A defeated foe. But God has given us power over the enemy, let's see how…

A Spirit of Discernment

First, He has given us a Spirit of discernment so that we are able to detect the presence of the enemy and recognize his schemes. We see him at work in other people, and we stand steadfastly to fight against him. Now remember, we are not fighting the people that he uses, we are fighting the spirit behind the person. When you understand the battle that you are fighting, then you know how to equip yourself for it. The enemy is not fighting us like he did 5 or maybe 10 years ago. He's not fighting us with stuff, he's fighting our minds. He's using situations and circumstances to put pressure on us mentally to drive us to suicide or insanity. If you're not thinking right, you can't behave right. If you can't behave right, you can't fight right. You must gird up the loins of your mind because this battle is personal to the enemy. His time is running out! Even in that, God has not left us without hope. He has given us His Word to know how to equip ourselves, even our minds to fight back against the attacks of the enemy. We need to get serious about this battle and stop taking it lightly. We need to pay attention to what is happening so that we won't be caught by surprise at the coming of the Lord. "For you know quite well that the day of the Lord's return will come unexpectedly, like a thief in

My Press to Praise

the night" (1 Thessalonians 5:2, NLT).

So in "Resolving to Endure" we need to strap up, or as the Word says, "**arm ourselves**."

1 Peter 4:1 "Forasmuch then
as Christ hath suffered for us in the flesh,
arm yourselves likewise with the same mind:
for he that hath suffered in the flesh
hath ceased from sin;
(2) That he no longer should live the rest of his time
in the flesh to the lusts of men,
but to the will of God."

When I looked up the word "resolve" on Google, it meant to **settle** or find a solution to a problem, dispute, or contentious matter. When I looked up the word endure, it meant to "**suffer** something painful or difficult **patiently**." Whew! So to "Resolve to Endure" you would need to settle in your mind first, that there is some suffering that must take place and I need a plan or be able to find a

solution for how I'm going to get through it!
SETTLING (in your mind) "Resolving" to
>SUFFER (through it) "Endure"

There are times that no matter how much you pray about a situation, God is silent. It never occurs to me that God is silent for a reason. I never even consider that because I just want what I want. So because He is silent, I then have to suffer through whatever I am facing until He decides to answer me. In the process of waiting, the Lord allows the heat of the trial to be so great that it begins to challenge you mentally. He's not trying to make you quit at this point, He is trying to make you produce. He is trying to extract out of your life what He knows is there. He knows what He has placed on the inside of you. But even in all of that, God is still not answering you. And just when you did not think that things could get any worse, some other unexpected thing happens and now you are at your breaking point, and you find yourself crying out to God violently for help! But God is still silent. What are you going to do? Here is where

My Press to Praise

God is supposed to get the glory out of your suffering. Either you are going to turn away from God or you're going to endure the suffering. If your choice is to "resolve" to suffering or to endure, you must choose how to do that. This is where your knowledge of the Word comes into play. Your situation is not changing, so you have the option of speaking to it and commanding it to move or continue to be silent and hope that something falls out of the sky. God has a unique way of applying pressure to your life that ultimately PRESSES you into Praise! I have learned that the more you pray God's Word back to Him, the more liberating you began to feel in what you're going through because "the Lord is the Spirit, and where the Spirit of the Lord is, there is liberty" (2 Corinthians 3:17).

When you invite God into your situation by agreeing with what His word says about it, it MUST change. It cannot remain the same. Knowing this, you can now choose to praise *in the middle* of that thing because you have believed the report of the Lord. You have learned how to settle in your mind that sink or swim, I'm going to plant my feet and stand with the Lord. So now you've come to a place of confidence in God that you can expect Him to move on your behalf regardless of the situation, because you understand that there is nothing too hard for Him. Therefore, the Lord reminds us in Matthew 6:5 that "when you pray, do not be like the hypocrites who love to stand and pray in the synagogues and on street corners so that other people can see them because I tell you the truth, they have received their reward in full." Matthew 6:6 says, "But when you pray (that's a whole message by itself) go into your room, close the door, and pray to your Father who is unseen. Then your Father, who sees what is done in secret, will reward you.

Now, let's go back to verse 6 because I want to make sure that I address this portion of scripture. It is important that we do not miss this. The verse begins by stating "but when you pray." This is to purposefully address you the individual, that you should not be so focused on what others are doing, but do what *you* are supposed to do. We spend the bulk of our lives trying to imitate what others are doing and sometimes we must fall in the ditch before we realize that we are following the wrong examples. Jesus is the example. Jesus said "I am the way, and the truth, and the life; no one comes to the Father, but through Me" (John 14:6). I remember spending a lot of my time watching other folks in church. If they had joy, I had joy. If they were sad, I was sad. I was just trying to understand their connection to the Lord because then I would have probably imitated that. One of the most valuable lessons that my leaders taught me early in my walk with the Lord, was to know the Lord for myself, to study to show myself approved before God. "Resolving to Endure" is a personal journey that you will have to take as an individual and nobody can walk this path but you. It's an individual mindset that you must adapt that's free from self-will and the opinions of those who have not been washed in the blood of the Lamb. It's a single-eyed view of the mark, a determination to

Teresa A. Stith

PRESS through to victory regardless of your situation.

"Brethren, I count not myself to have apprehended:

but this one thing I do,

forgetting those things which are behind,

and reaching forth

unto those things which are before,

I **press** toward the mark

for the prize of the high calling of God

in Christ Jesus"

(Philippians 4:13,14).

I like how Dr. Tony Evans says:

"In the natural if you see it

you believe it.

But in the spiritual, you believe it

and then you see it.

REMOVE the Stone!"

"Blessed are the pure in heart, for they will see God" (Matthew 5:8). To resolve to endure you must… get a new heart! ♥

Your APPROACH to Praise

(2)

Your approach to praise is contingent upon two very important things:
1. Who God is…and…
2. Who God is to you!

Being confident in these two things is what makes praise so rich! Regardless of the season of life you're in, all other things are irrelevant when you know the answer to these. You certainly cannot praise God if you don't know who He is, so what is your relationship with the Father looking like? You can only praise God as much as you know of Him. I can literally recall early in my walk with the Lord, how some of the older saints of God used to testify. I used to love testimony time because the older Mothers in the church would break out with a song and when the song was finished, a fiery testimony would follow. One Mother said, "you can't make me doubt Him because I know too much about Him!" Another would stand up and praise God and then get happy. Now what we meant by "getting happy" is that when the individual yields him or herself to the power of God, the Holy Spirit takes over. Because their worship and praise are so elevated, it causes them to lose all control of their natural selves and God is magnified in and through them. This oftentimes causes them to break out in a dance and then like a fire, it spreads throughout the congregation and people start popping up like popcorn to share what great things that God has done for them. Being a young girl in church at the time, I used to desire that. I wanted to praise God like that. I wanted to testify like that, but I couldn't because I didn't know God on that level yet. The Mothers used to call Jesus "a bridge over troubled water" and I'd be sitting there like… huh? The closer that I became to the Lord myself, I began to understand the terminology that some have used to describe what their relationship with the Lord has been like. To some, He's been a "Way Maker" and to others He's been "Peace" in the midst of the storms. When you know who God is to you, you can approach His throne with boldness and expectancy. You *expect* God to answer and *expect* Him to hear because you have grown to know how He operates and how He moves in the hearts of those who put their total trust in Him. An ole familiar hymnal says "I will enter His gates with thanksgiving in my heart, and I will enter His courts with praise…I will say this is the day that the Lord has made, I will rejoice for He has made me glad!" What we can take away from this song is that whether we are entering His gates or His courts, we must do so in a Spirit of praise! Why are we rejoicing? Why are we so glad? Your answer should be your approach to praise and to God as you are freely given the opportunity to come into His presence. Nobody else knows like you know what God has done for you. When you come into the presence of God, start right there. Think of all the wonderful things that God has given you the strength to overcome. Recall how He worked on your behalf when you did not know how a situation would end.

Remember how broken you were about the loss of someone close to you and how God gave you the strength to endure. When we focus our attention on these things that we normally would take for granted, we are learning about God and His character. We are understanding His love and how it covers a multitude of sins. Because God loves us even when we fail, He understands that we are frail in our own strength and He desires to help us. We must *want* the help that God wants to give. He urges us to ASK, and it shall be given to us, SEEK and we shall find, and KNOCK and the door will be opened unto us (Matthew 7:7-8). Don't allow the weight and guilt of sin to rob you of a relationship with the Lord or of your praise. God loves you even in your mess. He offers the gift of His Son Jesus Christ to you so that you don't have to stay in your current situation. You don't have to live like someone with no hope because HE IS your hope! You don't *have* to stay broken!

Every church service (it felt like) at some point, I would always break out with the song "I get joy

My Press to Praise

when I think about what He's done for me." I sung the song so much, I wondered if the other members were tired of hearing it because I certainly was not tired of singing it. Nobody understood the depth of the joy I felt when I sung that song because nobody knew like I knew what the Lord had done. It may had been hard for some to hear it, but it was easy for me to sing it because my heart was glad. Every time I approached God whether through singing, or sweeping off the church steps, I wanted Him to know how glad I was to do that for Him. I wanted Him to know how much I appreciated His presence in my life. I appreciated it so much that I was glad serve. I remember in the beginning when we were learning how to serve, we had gone to another church who had asked us to serve. My First Lady always taught us how to be women. Women of Strength. I remember we were all standing around at this event pretty much waiting for the guests to need something so that we could go and serve. We were ready and we were surely looking the part. Rather than waiting on the guests, I began to take a pitcher through the tables asking if anyone would like anything else to drink. I just began tending to the tables rather than waiting for them to call us. Some of my other sisters followed. That's when I learned the meaning of John 4:35:

> "Behold I say to you, look out into the fields
>
> for they are white already to harvest.
>
> For the harvest is plentiful
>
> but the laborers are few."

I understood that there will be many people who may not ever come to us maybe because of fear, shame, guilt, pride, whatever…but we should always be ready and willing to go to them. When we made ourselves available, the needs became evident. Everybody began asking for things. The same with God. When we approach His throne, even though He knows what our needs are, He urges us to come anyway. He compels us to ask anyway. He wants us to pray anyway. It is in this place of complete submissiveness where He empowers us and equips us to go out into the fields. The more you approach

His throne, the more you began to act like Him. The more you stay in His face and on your face, the more you began to look like Him. The more you think about Him, the more His life is reflected on you, and as you continue to die to yourself, the more He lives in and through you. So be careful how you approach God. He told Moses in Exodus 3:5…

> "And He said, Draw not nigh hither:
> put off thy shoes from off thy feet,
> for the place whereon thou standest
> is holy ground."

Consider More Approaches

If you woke up on the wrong side of the bed this morning, consider another approach before stepping into the presence of the Lord. From the time that you open your eyes in the morning, to the time that you bow your head to pray is enough time for you to get yourself together before approaching the throne of God. Now I'm not saying to be fake when you go to God in prayer, because sometimes we find ourselves on our knees because of brokenness and sadness. We are human. God is ALL POWERFUL and ALL-KNOWING and knowing this allows us to be able to carry our burdens to Him, and leave them there! We should never leave the presence of God the same way that we came. He, through the Holy Ghost, is able to revive us and give us encouragement so that we can revive, encourage, and pour into the lives of those around us. This is how others can find Him, through your life and testimony of God's grace and mercy toward you in your time of need.

God is a God of Order

First things first! Get your priorities straight. Get the order right. God…and then…everything else! One thing that I can honestly say that God has brought into my life is structure. If it had not been for Him, I would still be walking aimlessly around with no substance and without hope. There would be no sustainability on my part and nothing to even show for having lived on this earth for fifty plus years. God taught me how to value my life and how to have respect for myself and others. He changed my attitude and gave me a purpose for living. There were so many things that He taught me about myself and about others. He taught me how to handle situations and circumstances His way and not to act out of my flesh. He taught me how to execute judgement with mercy and how to show mercy to others even if I felt that they were undeserving of it because this is what He does for us daily. The more I learn about Him, the more that WHO HE IS becomes a part of me. Now, I can feel the power of His presence and almost instantaneously know what He's saying, or how He's going to move on a situation without Him ever having to say a Word! Have you ever had that experience? The Lord has taught me how to appreciate life and pay attention to things that we often overlook.

    One day I had the opportunity to watch a family of ants who were busy with their day. I remember thinking how small they were, yet every now and again, I would see one of them carrying a piece of a scrap of food that had fallen to the ground.

They seemed to be in a hurry as they scurried about in a sequence and then repeat their actions all over again. I laughed because I imagined that they had their own list of problems to deal with and just like us, were busy trying to make ends meet for their families. I will never know what it will be like to be an ant, but rather than just step on them when I see them, I had another appreciation for who they were. There's always a lesson to be learned and wisdom to gain if we would take the time to listen and pay attention. The answers that we need to maneuver this life are all around us, and if we spent more time praising and less time complaining, PRAISE would become rather easy for us!

How I learned this...

I just simply got tired of complaining! I was getting on my own nerves whining and complaining about every little thing. It had gotten to the point that I was giving myself migraine headaches because I was stressing about something that I could not change. Once I learned how to rightly apply the Word

My Press to Praise

of God to my situations, a lot of things in my life changed. It was really an eye opener for me. I had spent years allowing the enemy to bounce me up and down like a yo-yo and I felt powerless. One day it was like a lightbulb just literally popped on to let me know that I didn't have to accept these things! I didn't have to allow my thoughts to dictate how I would feel about my day. I didn't have to allow my thoughts to tell me how defeated I looked or that there was no hope for me because I could decide these things on my own. When negative thoughts bombarded my mind, I immediately cast them down to the ground and replaced them with what God said about them in the Word. This ultimately kept me hopeful and rooted and grounded in my faith. You can praise your way through every single obstacle that comes to test your faith when you stay focused on the promises of God and not on what you see in the natural. Remember, the whole world is without hope *without* the Lord, so why are we expecting anything in it to work properly? We shouldn't. We must learn to command things to change for us because Jesus gave us the power to do that! That's a right that we have as children of God. We can call those things that be not, as though they were (Romans 4:17). It's amazing how a simple change of heart or a change of mind about a thing will bring a whole slew of blessings into your life. When I chose to put the cares of this life into their proper place (in Jesus' hands) my health got better, and I was a much happier individual. You cannot praise God effectively when you are worried about things that you do not have the power to change. It's when you stop worrying and trust God, then His peace takes over. A friend of mine once told me "you don't let anything bother you." Little did he know, it took a LOT for me to get to this place in my life. It was not easy to let go of certain things especially when I had been in control of them for much of my life. I had to be taught how to yield these things to the Lord, and oftentimes after I had given them to Him, I would go back and pick them up again! It was a trying season for me, but eventually I made it over.

My Press to Praise

Your approach to praise is a time to yield, a time to reflect on God's Word and ask yourself, "what does all of this mean for me?" If your answer is not Jesus Christ, there's some more searching that you need to do because your approach to praise is all wrapped up in what took place on Calvary. Jesus hung, bled, and died for us all that day. When we were dead in our sins, without hope, he sacrificed his life. Took our sins upon himself and rescued us from eternal death and damnation. Whew! Think about this the next time the Pastor says "stand on your feet and let's give the Lord some praise up in here!" I can recall times that I heard that and couldn't give God praise because I was blinded by my situations. I didn't think that I should give God praise because I had issues that God had not worked out. Whew! The fact that God let me live through those moments because He understood my ignorance of the Word, my lack of understanding for the price that Jesus paid for me to even be standing there! Hallelujah!

You cannot approach God's throne with

baggage. We must lay aside *every* weight and let God renew our strength in His presence. In this place of yielding or approaching, allow yourself to become lost in WHO God is which in turn, releases you from relying on self, the world, or any other limited resource. You are trusting in His total provision for your life. You are saying "Father, I trust you with my life and I believe that you are fully aware of what my needs are, and fully capable of supplying them. I believe that you are making a way for me now. Continue to accomplish the things that You have sought to do in my life, and I give you all the glory!" Your approach to praise will not be the same as someone else's because you will only receive from God as much as you're willing to give of yourself to Him. SOOO…. learn how to yield.

My Press to Praise

The PRESS in Your Praise

(3)

For years now, the Lord has enabled me to share His goodness in my life with others through messages of faith and hope. I have two faith groups "Afaiththatworks" and "Faith It to Make It" both on Facebook along with several other platforms that I use to speak life into the lives of other people. There are times that I too, am tried and tested by the words that I give to others. So then, what is the PRESS in my praise? What keeps me coming back here time and time again? Praise is simply an outlet for me. It takes me to another place spiritually and it enables me to maintain my sanity amidst a dying and distracting world. I used to be so disappointed in God. Of course this was when I did not know any better. Situations and circumstances that I had to deal with in life just made me angry. The more I heard about God being "rich" and "the cattle upon a thousand hills belongs to Him," the angrier I became as I wondered why (if all of this is true) am I still struggling? If God has all of this, why isn't He giving me any of it?" Is this what's blocking *your* praise? Are you angry with God about something? Are you disappointed in God? Did He make you some promise that you still have not received? I'll tell you this, being angry with God will not get you what you're asking Him for. As a matter of fact, why should God rush to get you out of a mess that you clearly got yourself in? God does not care about you being angry and trying to seduce Him with tears and all of the pity parties. What He does care about is you understanding and learning who He is and what you need to do to make it to Heaven. That is His concern for you, that you be SAVED! He wants you to come to the knowledge of the truth so that you can spend eternity with Him. When you know who God is, you learn what He expects from you, and when you give Him what He desires, He in return, gives you what you desire. God will not bless you if you have unconfessed sin in your life, He will deal with that first. The problem that we often run into is that we want the blessings of God but we don't want to obey His instructions to receive them. We become upset with God because we want Him to not be so holy at times, so that we can satisfy our flesh and get what we want. I'm sorry but that is not going to happen. God will never stop being who He is to satisfy your fleshly desires, and He's certainly not going to lower His standards because you don't feel like making the adjustments in your life. Remember, it was for this very purpose that He sent His Son to die on the cross for us because we could not save our own selves. We need to get some control over our flesh because not having control is seriously affecting our praise! The Bible teaches us that one day is as a thousand years to the Lord (2 Peter 3:8) and God has a little bit more time than you do to wait for you to get in line with what His will is for your life. The sooner you do this, the more time you will have to enjoy the years that God has given you. So go on and lift those hands and praise God where you are, because no matter where we are on our journey,

He's STILL God!

HE IS GOD

AND HE IS GOOD!

I heard someone say that trusting God in the light is nothing, but try trusting Him in the dark, that is FAITH! The dark does not have to be something that happens at night, it could be a situation or circumstance that you have absolutely no control over. It could be some form of depression or grief. Whatever dark place you may find yourself, there is hope for you if you learn to praise your way through it. Your "press" to praise does not mean that you won't be hurt or troubled at the things that come to make us sad, it simply means that "in them" you're still able to recognize who God is. This is the PRESS, that you are still able to PRAISE God in the middle of your storms!

"Finally, brethren, whatever things are true, whatever things are noble, whatever things are just, whatever things are pure, whatever things are lovely, whatever things are of good report,

My Press to Praise

if there is any virtue

and if there is anything praiseworthy —

meditate on these things."

Philippians 4:8

Get OUT of Your Comfort Zone!

To "press" means that sometimes you must do something that is outside of what you would normally do if given the chance. Pressing means moving or causing to move into a position of contact with something (or Someone) by exerting continuous physical (Spiritual) force! I absolutely love that definition and of course, I needed it to have a more spiritual tone. When you "Press to Praise" you are choosing to (mentally) move yourself into a position of contact with our Heavenly Father by exerting continuous force (bombarding Heaven with your prayers) and vowing to not let go until the Lord blesses you (Read how Jacob wrestled with the angel of God in Genesis 32: 22-32). But let's also look at the woman with the issue of blood. We find her in

Teresa A. Stith

Matthew 5: 25-34. "The unnamed woman in this gospel story is a woman who has suffered for 12 years from a certain kind of bleeding, it is often translated as "hemorrhaging." She has visited many doctors and healers, and none of them has been able to heal her. As a matter of fact, the Bible states that she grew worse. It seems frenetic and like she is acting out in a last-ditch effort. Her very presence in a large crowd would be frowned upon in this society because she is considered "unclean." Her normal existence would often have been spent watching people skirt around her to avoid the possibility of contact. No brushing or touching or sharing friendly gestures on the path. She lived in isolation and would have been known for her uncleanliness" (Riepma, 2022). But on this particular day, when she had heard of Jesus, the woman came in the **press** behind and touched his garment. For she said, "If I may touch but his clothes, I shall be whole." Verse 29 in the chapter says "And straightway (right away) the fountain of her blood was dried up; and she felt in her body that she was healed of that plaque." See, she had to do something that was outside of what she would normally do, she was an outcast! She had no business there because she was considered unclean. But she positioned herself for the press, she settled in her mind and was prepared to suffer whatever she needed to suffer to obtain her healing. Most of us would have probably given up when we saw how large the crowd was.

A Baptist Evangelist and Teacher, Chaplain Oswald Chambers said this in his excerpt on "The Authority of Truth." He shares...

"It is essential that you give people the opportunity to

ACT on the truth of God.

The responsibility must be left with the individual-

you CANNOT act for him.

It must be his own deliberate act, but the evangelical

message should always LEAD HIM to ACTION!

Refusing to act leaves a person paralyzed, exactly

where he was previously. But once he acts, he is never

the same. It is the apparent folly of the truth that stands in the way of hundreds who have been convicted by the Spirit of God.

Once I press myself into action, I IMMEDIATELY begin to LIVE because anything less, is merely existing. The moments I truly live, are the moments when I act with my ENTIRE WILL!"

This woman was given an opportunity to act and she took it! She PRESSED! She believed in what she perceived and it resulted in her complete healing! It was her responsibility (not Jesus') to act on what she already knew. Nobody else could make that decision for her. As stated, the evangelical message should always lead *you* to action. It's hard to hear the true, unadulterated Word of God preached and remain the same. You won't. But *you* must act. When Jesus knocks on the door of your heart, *you* must open the door. Once *you press yourself* into action, you immediately begin to live and not just exist in the world. This woman acted with her entire will thrust upon Jesus and because of that, she was made whole!

Pressing to praise means **applying pressure** to your praise. Apply pressure to your praise until it manifests that thing that you've been praying for. Stop letting the devil rob you of your praise to the Lord and continue to praise God whether you *feel* like it or not. You can't praise and you certainly cannot grow when you are in a place of comfort. Sometimes the Lord will apply pressure to your life because He is trying to extract something from it that will cause good things to flow into it. When your praise is bound, your fruit will wither. You cannot prosper fully when there's no joy in your life and your fruit will eventually dry up and die! A simple *sacrifice* of praise can truly change all of that. A heart that is truly surrendered to the Lord is one that prays and waits for God to answer, and one that *wants* to praise the Lord for His wonderful works.

We must decide that no matter what we are faced with or what we must endure, we will give to the Lord what is rightfully His…our praise! God should not be on punishment because we had a bad day or things did not go as planned in our lives. Faith in the promises of God should make us run on a little further. We must learn how to stand up in the face of adversity and tell the devil that because God has been so good to us, we will persist to praising our way through. "If we draw near to God, He will draw near to us" (James 4:8). What we don't give up for God, we will end up losing anyway. God promises us protection throughout the Bible so why do we underestimate those promises? God is not a liar. If He promises us something, He will fulfill what He said. God loves and cares for us and we must learn to live in that reality. God *is* interested in our lives.

> "Don't wait for your feelings
> to validate a truth that
> you should already know
> BY FAITH
> based on the Word of God!"
> -David "Diga" Hernandez

Make TIME to Praise
(4)

We make time or take time for everything else that we want to do, so why is it so hard to set aside time for God? Do we think that He is boring? What is it? Are we ashamed to come before His presence? If we feel this way, it is an indication that *maybe* we need to "Press" in a little harder. God gives us many opportunities to seek Him and find Him. He is not hiding from us. If we were not so busy, we would be able to hear Him more clearly, recognize when He's leading us and know which directions to take because we've spent time in His presence. The Holy Spirit pulls us into fellowship with the Father when we submit ourselves to His Lordship. If you have not developed a consistent prayer life with the Lord, it is not too late. There's no right or wrong way to approach the throne of God, however, practicing to respect the fact that He is a holy God is a start. Learn to acknowledge God for being God first and then humble yourself and honor the fact that He has allowed you into His presence. In today's world, the reverence for God is missing. He is holy. You can't try to handle God like you handle these worldly things in the world. When you step into the presence of God, you immediately bow yourself to show the Lord that you respect His position and authority and that you are fully aware of your own. He is God. We have no power, except God gives it to us so we must remain humble when approaching the throne of God. There seems to be a misconception that God is just waiting to hit us across the head with the Word due to our shortcomings, but that is so far from the truth. Yes, God is holy, and yes, He has standards, conditions, and instructions in righteousness that He requires us to follow. But God loves us first and He realizes that we are but clay and that without the power of the Holy Spirit living and moving on the inside of us, we cannot meet these conditions or requirements so He gives us a choice to be saved. Once you give your life to Christ, ALL the benefits of the Kingdom belong to you, and you are equipped with what you need to live a successful life through Christ. Don't try to hide from the Lord, but be honest about what you are needing from Him, He already knows anyway, but He respects our honesty and He will grant your desires when you approach Him with a sincere heart and in accordance with His will for your life. If you are having trouble setting aside time for the Lord, ask Him to show you when will be a good time for you and then be consistent with keeping covenant with God. Make it a habit to meet the Lord each day in the place that you have chosen. You will find that as you are consistent in returning to that place, that God will be there waiting for you. You will begin to feel His presence when you enter, and you will know that He is delighted to have you share your heart with Him. Be open to hear what the Lord has to say. Read the Word and wait for God to speak. He speaks differently to different people so make sure that you quiet yourself and not try so hard to hear *something* that you miss everything that He is saying.

God will move on your heart, and you will understand clearly what the Lord has said. Always seek forgiveness for yourself and others. You are just confessing to God that you realize that you have faults and may fail Him daily, but you are trying, and you need His grace to help you. God understands. We are not perfect people out here, but letting God know that we desire to be what He wants us to be allows Him the freedom that He needs to come in and help. Remember, He will not force His way into your heart or your life, He wants to be invited in. God is a loving Father who yearns for a relationship with us. He wants us to talk to Him. He wants to know how we are doing. He wants to conversate and communicate with us. He wants to know all about our day. If we stop thinking that He is so holy that He cannot meet us on our level, then our understanding of who He is will increase. We can truly love God when we truly KNOW Him. The Bible tells us that "Jesus was tempted in all points as we were, yet without sin" (Hebrews 4:15). In other words, you can't go through or experience anything in life, that God Himself through Jesus Christ has not already experienced. If you're not giving your time to Him, then what exactly are you doing with it? This is a very important question and you must be able to answer it.

A Good Choice or a God Choice?

I have used this phrase rather loosely when referring to singles who may be looking for a husband or wife but consider that it applies to much more than that. The choices that we make daily tend to not only affect our lives, but also those around us. To know if we are making good God choices should be prevalent to those of us who love the Lord. It is imperative that we understand the choices that we are making and that we are motivated by the Spirit of God in us to do so. Therefore, our time with the Lord in prayer is so very vital to our walk with the Lord. The Word reminds us to "in all of our ways acknowledge God and He will direct our paths" (Proverbs 3:6). So again, how we choose to use our time is contingent upon the relationship that we have established with the Lord and the practices that are put in place to groom it. Making time to praise requires sacrifice. A good God choice will teach us that sometimes we may have to give up something to get what we want and need from the Lord. How can God hear and answer your prayers if you have not taken the time to pray? We must learn how to fight against the opposition that comes to steal God's time away from us. PRESS IN harder when this happens! Your Spirit may be screaming for you to fall on your knees in prayer but your flesh may be screaming louder that you are tired and just want to lie down, which one will you obey? It is very important that you are able to recognize these distractions from the enemy and stand firm on the Word of God. It is in moments such as this that you should be able to tell your flesh that "yes, I may be tired, and I really want to lie down right now, but **first** I am going to humble myself before God and thank Him for giving me the strength that I needed to do all that I was able to do today. If it was not for Him, I can recall several times that I would not have made it through the day". This is how you overcome the flesh and negative thoughts when they try to steal God's glory from you. You PRESS in and say, "hallelujah anyhow!" and proceed to obey the voice of the Lord.

Why Spend Time with God?

The Lord knows that we have an adversary the devil whose main job is to distract us from living and doing things that pleases God. He wants us to curse God and not rely on God to fight our battles. He whispers things to us like "what do you need God for? You can do that yourself!" or why are you waiting on God? By the time He answers, it will be too late! If we entertained those thoughts that the enemy often bombard our minds with, we would begin to question God and doubt that He will come through. Then we began to start looking to the world for resources and we give in to what we think is right. This is how we error from the truth. We never give the Lord time to work things out for us and even if we did, we really don't believe that God can do what we're asking. So as much as the Lord wants to answer your prayers when you pray, He still can't because of unbelief. We often wonder why God is taking so long to answer us and it's because we do not believe that He will and unbelief my friends, is a sin!

If we look at the book of Jeremiah, he was known by some as "the weeping Prophet." Why do you think this was? Jeremiah's messages were those of hope and warning. The Israelites were getting away from their destiny and God was trying to call them back to Him. Jeremiah was very young when the Lord called him to the ministry. He was loved by God and he was faithful. The Lord challenged Jeremiah to execute His word to the children of Israel and the Prophet often wept because **his heart was so tender toward this people**. Jeremiah persevered through discouragement to deliver God's message. He *made time* to spend in the presence of the Lord.

PRAISE IS WHAT I DO or...*IS IT?*

There are so many voices that are consistently trying

My Press to Praise

to compete for our attention and distract us, but Jeremiah was not distracted. He stayed focused on the task at hand and obeyed the voice of the Lord. Here's a well-known passage of scripture from his book:

> "For I know the plans I have for you,
> declares the Lord,
> plans for welfare and not for evil
> to give you a future and a hope.
> Then you will call upon me and come and pray to me
> and I will hear you.
> You will seek me and find me
> when you seek me with all your heart."
> -Jeremiah 29:11-13:

Let us be reminded that there is an assignment that is on our lives and God created us to give Him glory. He stands at the door of our hearts, and He knocks. Will we open the door and let Him in?

Teresa A. Stith

Tamela Mann sings a song that goes something like this… ♫♫♫

> Change me O' God
>
> Make me more like You
>
> Change me O' God
>
> Wash me through and through
>
> Just create in me
>
> A clean heart
>
> So that I
>
> I can worship… worship You.

We can only make time for the Lord when we allow Him to change us.

My Press to Praise

A SHIFT in Worship and Praise
(5)

If you know me, then you'd also know that I love music. I have been singing since I was a young girl in the woods in a small town in Brunswick County, Virginia called Freeman. I remember when my father seemed to be so intrigued with my singing that he would call me to his bedroom door and have me stand at the door and sing for him and his girlfriend. He would call out to me, "Ree, come in here and sing that song for me by Betty Wright." I smile as I recall, and I would come running because I knew that I could sing, and I loved Betty Wright. I knew all of her songs (laugh out loud). His girlfriend liked my singing so much that she began to teach me and my siblings church songs. We'd learn the songs and when my grandparents took us to church, we would sing. We were called the "Stith Family" and we would sing our hearts out at a little church called Union Bethel. This brings back so many memories for me because although we could sing, I'm not sure if any of us understood at the time, what we were really singing about, BUT GOD! He heard us, watched over us, and protected us at such a young age when our lives seemed to be so unstable. Needless to say, that we are All involved in some aspect of the ministry now, and we just love God!

    Recently though, maybe the last few months, I've noticed that there has been a shift in my praise and worship. When I get in my vehicle, whether I am traveling or relaxing, the radio was usually the first thing that I'd adjust. Now I am finding myself sitting or riding in silence. I guess you are wondering, "what changed?" When I think about it, I think that my song preferences changed. Meaning that, the closer I became to the Lord, those random songs that I used to like didn't seem to resonate with my Spirit anymore. They began to sound like a bunch of clashing noise to me, like I could not find the significance in them. I've learned that whatever we are doing in the earth, must point us back to Christ because it's all about Him!

My Press to Praise

Beware of song choices that put you back in a spirit of defeat! Sometimes we get so carried away with a beat, that we are not really paying attention to what is being said and we're singing ourselves right back into bondage. I began to be drawn to songs that would push me into the presence of the Lord. Songs that would make me dig deeper to know God and connect my Spirit with His. Songs that would send me straight to my knees in worship and communication with my Heavenly Father. There is a difference. Being cognizant of this, I've had to listen intentionally for the voice of the Lord as His Spirit led me into another realm of His holiness. My ultimate desire then, became to "give Him glory." It became easy to do once I figured this out, and it became *all* I wanted to do. Other things around me began to not matter so much because I knew that God would handle those things for me. I had to stay in a Spirit of praise. *My heart changed.*

    Listen, you will know when the shift has come. You will not be the same. The people around you will know. They might not acknowledge it, but they will know. Don't worry about how they will perceive you, they will feel like you are acting brand new, but it won't be you at all, it will be God changing your countenance. It will be God elevating you and taking you to another level in Him. All that you have had to suffer through was not for naught because God knew what He was doing. All that you endured, *had* to happen so that God could bring you into this place. Imagine where you would be if you had not dared to step out on faith and move! It was your own obedience to God that has brought you to this place. You are about to give birth to something so big. There were people who thought that God had abandoned you and shut up your womb, but you are about to give birth and everyone is going to see this baby. Hallelujah! There was a process of conditioning that you had to endure before God could present you to the world, but the time has come. God is about to show you why you had to suffer through those seasons, why you had to be by yourself, why you had to go through those things alone. He's about to show you why He had to separate you, because what you were carrying, you could not birth until you completely understood the assignment and got into your position. God is about to reveal to you who you really are! You haven't even understood yourself, the calling that is upon your life, but God is about to release you. Let Him release you. We need to make sure that we are following God and His leading of us into worship. Pay attention to the transition, to the shift and conduct yourself accordingly.

A shift in worship comes from a "heart" of worship. If we go back to the dream in the beginning of the book, we will see "perfect" hearts of gold dancing along the sky, and at the Lord's command, formed this phrase: "Where is My Praise?" Worship belongs to the Lord. Praise belongs to the Lord. Glory belongs to the Lord. Sometimes we tend to look for these things in other people, places, or things, but God is the only one to whom worship is due. As stated, worship is more than just listening to our favorite songs, or participating in a worship service, or admiring the beauty of a thing. Worship has nothing to do with our individual styles or preferences, but it's all about our hearts. The Bible tells us to worship the Lord with "clean hands and a pure heart" (Psalm 24:4). The Bible also tells us in Matthew 15:8 (KJV) that "this people draweth nigh unto me with their mouth, and honoureth me with their lips; but their heart is far from me." Isaiah 29:13 (KJV) says "But in vain they do worship me, teaching for doctrines the commandments of men." What is the Lord saying in these verses? He is simply saying that our worship of Him is nothing but rules taught by men. In other words, like everything else, we have been taught how to make something that is not real, appear real and that's why God looks on our hearts. We have gotten good at lying and even going as far as to believe our own lies, but God sees all of these things. We need to ask God to "give us a heart like Thine?" That we might worship you and praise you as you deserve, and then we must commit to worship.

Plugged Into the Power

  You cannot have a shift in praise if you are not connected to the Power Source (God). Connection does not come from just "looking back over our lives." Being plugged into the power comes from a constant connection to the Spirit of God in you. This is what charges you, what fuels you. This is where you obtain mercy and find grace to help in your time of need (Hebrews 4:16, KJV). You can only give the Lord what you have and what you have depends on how much time you have spent in His presence, at His table, in His Word. It is in the Word that we find life. The Bible tells us that "the entrance of thy Words giveth light; It giveth understanding to the simple" (Psalm 119:130). The Lord has not made finding Him complicated for He states in John 1:4, "In him was life; and the life was the light of men." He goes on to say in John 4:16 that "I am the way, the truth, and the life: no man cometh unto the Father, but by me." So, to sum all of this up, it starts with and ends with Jesus! For **"salvation is found in NO ONE ELSE, for there**

is no other name under Heaven given to mankind by which we must be saved." Period.

John 1:12 states "But as many as received Him, to them gave he power to become the sons of God, even to them that believe on His name. So as we can see, the shift begins with our acceptance of Jesus Christ and the finished work on the cross. Until you can understand this, your praise may be hindered. This is the root of our praise. That Jesus gave up His life to reconcile us back to God. Whew! Listen… when you plug a power cord into an outlet, you know that you are connected because the thing that you plugged up begins to show some signs of life, right? It begins to work. If you put that same power cord into the outlet but did not push it all the way in, it cannot get the right connection and therefore does not work properly. As a matter of fact, if left unattended for a long period of time, could have the potential to start a fire. "A bad connection, outdated wiring, or a tripped circuit breaker can cause a malfunctioning outlet. But there are instances where only half of an electrical outlet works and the other one doesn't. It can happen for multiple reasons, and it is wise to call an electrician to look into the issue" (Zimmerman Electric Company, 2022). It is the same with the Lord. When you are truly connected to the **Right Source** of power, you will obviously begin to show some signs of life. You are able to function mentally, physically, and spiritually and walk *confidently* in the gifts and callings that God has purposed for your life. However, if you are connected halfway, some of the time, or only when you feel like it, you cannot get the right connection and if left unattended long enough, you'd eventually dry up and die. As a matter of fact, a bad connection could be summed up as distractions, self-righteousness, your will, straddling the fence, etc. The Lord makes it very clear in Revelation chapter 3:1 when He was addressing the church at Sardis. He said, "I know thy works (He sees what they were doing) that thou hast a name that thou livest, and art dead." Meaning that the church had all of the characterizations of one who was alive, but they were dead. They were virtually dead in spirit and in works. Like dead men walking. But to those who were believing and who were worthy, He told them to strengthen the things that remained. Then He went on to tell the church at Laodicea (verses 15 & 16) that "I know thy works, that thou art neither cold nor hot: I would thou wert cold or hot. So then because thou art lukewarm, and neither cold nor hot, I will spue thee out of my mouth." We need to understand that this church was virtually worthless because they lacked genuine faith. Although they were known to be a wealthy place, spiritually the people of the church were poor, blind, and naked because true wealth was found only in God's grace. Are you plugged into the power?

Get a New HEART

(6)

When it's all said and done, ask God to give you a new heart. We want to have hearts that are going to obey God, honor Him, worship Him, and give Him the glory that is due His name. Our hearts are deceitful, we don't even know all that is in our own hearts. We do not understand all that we are capable of unless God reveals these things to us. The Word says "the heart *is* deceitful above all things, and desperately wicked: who can know it?" (Jeremiah 17:9). Let me share with you some of the benefits of having a new heart according to the Word of God.

1. You will begin to love what God loves
2. You will hate what God hates
3. You will acknowledge God in all your ways
4. You will want to please Him
5. You will love others even if they hate you
6. You will reverence the Lord
7. You will tell others about God
8. You will delight in God's Word
9. You will not try to hide from God
10. You will want to walk in your destiny

AND so much more! These are only a FEW of the benefits of being in Christ and having a heart like His. Jesus says in John 15 (NIV) …

"I am the vine; you are the branches.

If a man remains in me and I in him,

he will bear much fruit; apart form me

you can do nothing.

If anyone does not remain in me, he is like a branch

that is thrown away and withers;

such branches are picked up, thrown into the fire

and burned."

God is our Power Source and Jesus is how we connect with Him. Only the pure in heart will see God.

My Press to Praise

We are required as children of God to live a certain lifestyle. It is not an option. It is mandatory for us to live by the Word of God every day. When God is in control, we are not! Having a new heart assures us that the gospel message about Jesus will be shared with those in our circles. Jesus Christ is Lord and He is presently ALIVE and ACTIVE in Heaven! He continues to actively guide and advocate for us. As disciples of His, we must reflect His life and His love in all that we do, all that we say, whether we are on or off the job. Our attitudes and behaviors should mirror His life in such a way that we are able to point others to the cross. The character of our Father in Heaven should be reflected in our hearts and people should know straightway that there is something different about us, the way we handle situations and the way in which we respond to others. We are in the world, not of the world however, we are still tempted by things in the world. We are still human, and we are still wrapped in flesh. Christ makes the difference in our lives. We no longer handle situations and circumstances as someone who does not know the Lord.

Worship in Spirit and in TRUTH

God's Word makes it easy for us to PRESS on into PRAISE. When we grasp the understanding of why we are here, everything else becomes easy. It's just a matter of recalling the things that God has said. As long as we are alive and on this earth, we will battle thoughts, and distractions, and fight really hard to avoid people, places, and things that are destined and designed to pull us away from the things of God. We can take power over those temptations by rightly applying the Word of God to those situations. The more we press in, the more we become dependent and reliant upon God to supply our needs. Pretty soon just like a baby, we have learned how to stand up and walk on our own. We stop looking for worldly resources and we hold firm to the promises of God. What a beautiful love story. The Lord loves us so much that He was willing when He left the earth to send us "another Comforter" the Holy Ghost who He said would teach us all things and bring back to our remembrance those things that we have been taught. (John 14:26). The Lord has never left us alone. When I look back over my life, I remember wondering if I would ever figure this thing out. I wondered if I would ever get to a place where I solely trusted in the Lord and that was enough for me. I wanted to grow to a place of absolute faith and expectation in God. I wanted to *confidently* rely on Him and not anyone or anything else. O' me of little faith. I did not realize then just how much God loved me, and that He would never begin a work in me and not complete it or bring it to fruition. He has kept His word. He has watched over His word in my life, that it might perform that which He has sent it to do. I have power! I've had it all along, I was just afraid that it wouldn't work if I tried it. Shame on me.

    My faith in the Word of God is what makes the Word work. God is not a God that sits in Heaven and picks and chooses which of His children He's going to bless today. He told the blind men in Matthew 9: 28-

29, "Believe ye that I am able to do this? They said unto him, Yea, Lord. Then touched He their eyes saying, according to your faith be it unto you." He has given us all a measure of faith. How you use your measure is entirely up to you, but to get results, the Word must be spoken in faith because "without faith, it is impossible to please the Lord" (Hebrews 11:6). This has truly been a journey. Bless the name of the Lord for all the wonderful things that we are enjoying right now, and those which are to come. But most importantly, because our names have been written in the Lamb's Book of Life. Amen.

My Press to Praise

Now THINK on These Things
(7)

To PRESS into PRAISE, I will leave you with these scripture passages that will challenge you to change the way that you think. What you must remember is that we are supposed to have the mind of Christ. That means that regardless of how the wind blows in our lives, we should be responding like Christ would. You may be saying, "well I'm not Jesus." While I know that this is true, I also know that He has given us power! Jesus said in John 14:12 (NLT) "I tell you the truth, anyone who believes in me will do the same works I have done, and even *greater* works, because I am going to be with the Father." The key to your being able to live this life successfully is faith in the Words that the Lord has spoken. Jesus says that "the Words that I speak unto you, they are spirit, and they are life" (John 6:63). This means that the actual Word of God is Spirit! That is why it is referred to as "the Living Word" because it is ALIVE.

Teresa A. Stith

"When you release the Word of God, you are literally releasing the life-giving Spirit of God that will then do exceedingly abundantly above whatever it is that you are asking or thinking according to the power that is at work in you!" (Spirit Food, 2022) (Ephesians 3:20).

Let's GO IN!

Lord, You are my God;
I will exalt you and praise your name,
for in perfect faithfulness
you have done wonderful things,
things planned long ago.
Isaiah 25:1

The Lord is my strength and my shield;
my heart trusts in Him, and He helps me.
My heart leaps for joy,
and with my song I praise Him.
Psalm 28:7

My Press to Praise

Let everything that has breath praise the Lord.

Praise the Lord.

Psalm 150:6

Because your love is better than life,

my lips will glorify you.

I will praise you as long as I live,

and in Your name I will lift up my hands.

Psalm 63:3-4

Why, my soul, are you downcast?

Why so disturbed within me?

Put your hope in God

for I will yet praise Him

my Savior and my God.

Psalm 42:11

Great is the Lord and most worthy of praise;

His greatness no one can fathom.

Psalm 145:3

Teresa A. Stith

For you created my inmost being;

You knit me together in my mother's womb.

I praise You because I am fearfully

and wonderfully made;

Your works are wonderful, I know that full well.

Psalm 139:13-14

My mouth is filled with Your praise,

declaring Your splendor all day long.

Psalm 71:8

I will bless the Lord at all times; His praise shall

continually be in my mouth.

Psalm 34:1

Let the message of Christ dwell among you richly

as you teach and admonish one another

with all wisdom through psalms

hymns, and songs from the Spirit

singing to God with gratitude in your hearts.

Colossians 3:16

My Press to Praise

It's hard to appreciate the wine if you don't understand the process of the grapes!

Teresa A. Stith

For Thought:

I had a dream, and in the dream, I saw gold hearts floating across the sky. These weren't just any ole' hearts, they were *perfect* gold hearts and each one was clothed with fire. One after another, they floated in sync with each other along the sky. I was absolutely amazed, as I had never seen a *perfect heart* before. Suddenly, there appeared a man whom I perceived to be Christ or One like the Son of man, who stepped out from behind the clouds and gave a command by raising his right hand. When He raised his right hand, those hearts began to race across the sky (still in sync with one another) and then forming this phrase **"WHERE IS MY PRAISE?"**

About the Author

Blessings in the name of our Lord and Savior Jesus Christ. Teresa is an Author of Faith who lives to motivate, inspire, and build others up in the area of their faith. Her love and compassion for faith inspires others in such a way that it ultimately moves them into divine fellowship and relationship with the Lord. Regardless of her readers situations and circumstances, she thrives on helping them to find solutions for them in the Word of God. She gives them hope and enables them to discover (in themselves) the power and the confidence that they need to achieve and walk in victory.

She has over 20 years of experience in State Government where she has held many leadership titles and roles from Food Service Supervisor to Corrections Captain, to Certified General Instructor to Subject Matter Specialist to Dialogue Coach to Deputy Sheriff to her most recent position as Correctional Counselor 2. She was inducted into the National Society of Leadership and Success and a 2022 ACHI Award Magazine Nominee. She currently has an Associate's and Bachelor's Degree in Criminal Justice and enrolled in the Master's Program seeking a degree in Industrial Organizational Psychology. This is her 7th self-published title. Follow and connect with her to learn more.

Teresa A. Stith

My Press to Praise

New and Upcoming Titles

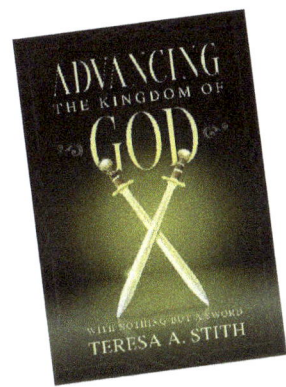

Teresa A. Stith

Follow Me

Facebook

Teresa Stith

Love Psalms to God For My Husband

Faith It To Make It

Afaiththatworks

Author/Writer/Publisher-Teresa Stith

Faith It To Make It 2

Instagram

Afaiththatworks

LinkedIn

Teresa Stith

TikTok

teresastith436

Website: afaiththatworks.com

Email: afaiththatworks@outlook.com

Online Store: faith-it-to-make-it.company.site

TERESA A. STITH
AN "AUTHOR OF FAITH"

- PUBLIC SPEAKER
- MOCK INTERVIEWER
- MENTOR
- FAITH ADVOCATE
- LIFE COACH
- COUNSELOR
- & MORE

FROM DISTRACTION TO DESTRUCTION TO DELIVERANCE!

CONTACT FOR SPEAKING ENGAGEMENTS AT:
AFAITHTHATWORKS@OUTLOOK.COM

References

Chambers, Oswald. (2022). *My Utmost for His Highest. The Authority of Truth.* Retrieved from https://utmost.org/the-authority-of-truth/

Photo Credit. *Fermentation.* (2021, January 11). CK12. https://k12.libretexts.org/@go/page/13282

Photo Credit. *A New Heart.* Johnson, Jeff Philip. (2017). Retrieved from http://www.youtube.com/@philipjeffjohnson1900

Riepma, Alisha. (2022). *The Woman Who Bled for 12 Years.* Retrieved from https://www.faithward.org/the-woman-who-bled-for-12-years/

Spirit Food. (2022). *The Word of God is Spirit and it is Life.* Retrieved from https://myspiritfood.org/pastors-devotionals/the-word-of-god-is-spirit-and-it-is-life/

Zimmerman Electric Company. (2022). *When Only One Half of An Outlet Works.* Retrieved from https://www.zimmermanelectricco.com/surprise-az-electrician-blog/when-only-one-half-of-an-outlet-works

www.ingramcontent.com/pod-product-compliance
Lightning Source LLC
Chambersburg PA
CBHW070938160426
43193CB00011B/1735